D1272377

COUNTRY PROFILES

GERMANY

BY AMY RECHNER

BELLWETHER MEDIA • MINNEAPOLIS, MN

Blastoff! Discovery launches a new mission: reading to learn. Filled with facts and features, each book offers you an exciting new world to explore!

This edition first published in 2018 by Bellwether Media, Inc.

No part of this publication may be reproduced in whole or in part without written permission of the publisher.
For information regarding permission, write to Bellwether Media, Inc.,
Attention: Permissions Department,
5357 Penn Avenue South, Minneapolis, MN 55419.

Library of Congress Cataloging-in-Publication Data

Names: Rechner, Amy, author.
Title: Germany / by Amy Rechner.
Description: Minneapolis, MN : Bellwether Media, Inc., 2018. |
    Series: Blastoff! Discovery: Country Profiles |
    Includes bibliographical references and index. |
    Audience: Age: 7-13.
Identifiers: LCCN 2017031933 (print) | LCCN 2017032978 (ebook)
    | ISBN 9781626177321 (hardcover : alk. paper) |
    ISBN 9781681034867 (ebook)
Subjects: LCSH: Germany–Juvenile literature.
Classification: LCC DD17 (ebook) | LCC DD17 .R427 2018 (print) |
DDC 943–dc23
LC record available at https://lccn.loc.gov/2017031933

Editor: Paige V. Polinsky   Designer: Brittany McIntosh

Printed in the United States of America, North Mankato, MN.

TABLE OF CONTENTS

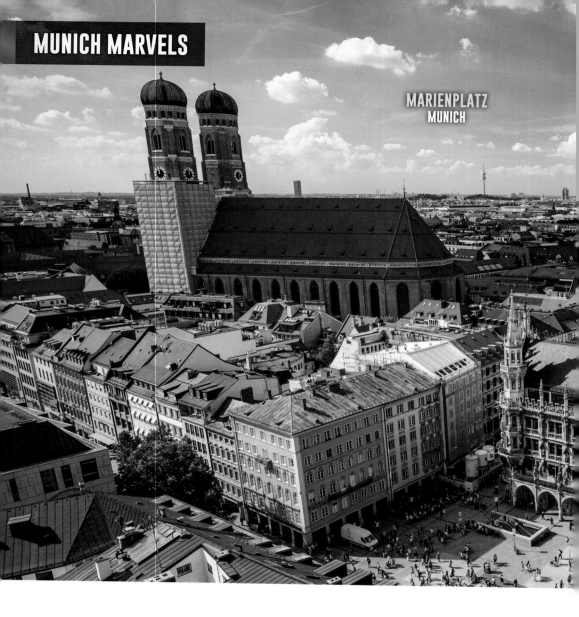

MARIENPLATZ
MUNICH

A family arrives in Munich, Germany. They walk along wide, beautiful streets lined with ancient buildings. They explore the Munich Residenz, Germany's largest city castle. The former palace is now a museum full of **elegant** paintings and furniture.

OTHER TOP SITES

BRANDENBURG GATE

COLOGNE CATHEDRAL

NEUSCHWANSTEIN CASTLE

NUREMBERG CASTLE

After enjoying a hot pretzel in the public gardens, the family wanders over to Marienplatz. This **medieval** town square has existed since 1158. They sit at an outdoor café like true *Müncheners*, or Munich locals. The sun begins to set while street musicians perform. The green domes atop the Church of Our Lady glow in the dusky light. Welcome to Germany!

LOCATION

Germany is a country in central Europe. It is a little smaller than the state of Montana, covering 137,847 square miles (357,022 square kilometers). Its capital, Berlin, sits on the country's northeastern side.

The Netherlands, Belgium, Luxembourg, and France line Germany's western border. To the north are the North Sea, Denmark, and the Baltic Sea. Poland and the Czech Republic lie to the east. Germany's southern border is shared by Switzerland and Austria. The Alps mountain range and Lake Constance line this border.

NORTH SEA

NETHERLANDS - - - -

BELGIUM

FRANCE

DENMARK

BALTIC
SEA

HAMBURG

BERLIN

POLAND

COLOGNE

GERMANY

FRANKFURT

UXEMBOURG

CZECH
REPUBLIC

MUNICH

LAKE
CONSTANCE

AUSTRIA

SWITZERLAND

A large **plain** stretches over northern Germany. **Marshes** line the country's western coast. In the south, the Black Forest carpets hills and valleys. These hills become mountains in the Bavarian Alps as they approach the southern border. Zugspitze, the country's tallest mountain, stands 9,718 feet (2,962 meters) among them.

RHINE RIVER

ZUGSPITZE ▲

■ = BLACK FOREST   ■ = BAVARIAN ALPS

BLACK FOREST
BADEN-WÜRTTEMBERG

ZUGSPITZE

BERLIN

Average seasonal highs and lows

JANUARY
HIGH: 35 °F (2 °C)
LOW: 27 °F (-3 °C)

APRIL
HIGH: 56 °F (13 °C)
LOW: 39 °F (4 °C)

JULY
HIGH: 74 °F (23 °C)
LOW: 55 °F (13 °C)

OCTOBER
HIGH: 56 °F (13 °C)
LOW: 43 °F (6 °C)

°F = degrees Fahrenheit
°C = degrees Celsius

Germany's rivers mostly flow north into the Baltic or North Sea. The Rhine, its longest river, spans the entire western side. Germany's climate is **temperate** with cold winters and cool summers. Rain and snow are plentiful in the north and high in the mountains.

Germany has many kinds of wildlife. Its marshes and rivers are home to beavers and muskrats. Wild boars snuffle through woodlands in search of roots and bugs. Germany's southern forests and mountains house goat-like chamois.

In the winter, Germany hosts thousands of **hibernating** bats. They fly out of the Kalkberg mountain caves and other nearby sites each spring. Meanwhile, starlings, thrushes, and sparrows dart across the country's plains. Falcons swoop from mountaintops to seize prey. Germany's official **symbol**, the golden eagle, nests high in the Alps.

GREATER MOUSE-EARED BAT

CHAMOIS

GRAY SEAL PUP

GOLDEN EAGLE

KILLER CUTIES

Gray seal pups have some of the cutest baby faces in the world. But do not be fooled. As adults, they are Germany's largest predator.

WILD BOAR

WILD BOAR

Life Span: 10 years
Red List Status: least concern

wild boar range = ▮

LEAST CONCERN	NEAR THREATENED	VULNERABLE	ENDANGERED	CRITICALLY ENDANGERED	EXTINCT IN THE WILD	EXTINCT

More than 80 million people live in Germany. It has the second-largest population in Europe. Most residents are **native** Germans. Some are **immigrants** from Turkey or other nearby European countries. The official language is standard German. Local **dialects** are still very common.

Christianity is the top religion in Germany. Most of the country's Christians are either Catholic or Protestant. A small number of Germans are Muslim or Jewish. Many do not practice any religion.

FAMOUS FACE

Name: Angela Merkel
Birthday: July 17, 1954
Hometown: Hamburg, Germany
Famous for: First female chancellor of Germany and winner of the U.S. Presidential Medal of Freedom in 2011

SPEAK GERMAN

ENGLISH	GERMAN	HOW TO SAY IT
hello	hallo	HA-lo
goodbye	auf wiedersehen	owf VEE-der-zane
please	bitte	BIT-eh
thank you	danke	DAHNK-eh
yes	ja	YAH
no	nein	NINE

FRANKFURT

COMMUNITIES

Most Germans live near large cities. Families are small, with one or two children. Many couples choose not to have children at all. Germany also has a large number of unmarried and elderly people.

NUREMBERG

OPEN HOUSE

Since Germany has more seniors than young people, a new kind of shared housing has begun. These homes are shared by elderly people and young families. They create new friendships and communities that care for each other.

U-BAHN
IN HAMBURG

City housing is expensive. People often rent small apartments in high-rise buildings. They use public transportation like the U-Bahn system to get around. Townhouses and single-family homes line tidy streets outside of big cities. The country is linked by its superfast highway, the Autobahn. It has firm driving rules, but only certain areas have speed limits.

A DOG'S LIFE

German dogs have good manners, too. In some cities, each dog must be trained and pass a test before going home with its owner. Barking, biting, and running off are not allowed!

Germans are considered very formal people. Children are taught to be respectful and on time. Jokes and laid-back talks are shared with friends and family. New friendships can take a while to build.

German people work hard and keep their busy lives organized. They like order and structure. Many towns have rules to keep daily life enjoyable. Neighborhoods often observe quiet time beginning at 10 p.m. every night. Shops close on Sundays so everyone can enjoy a day of rest and family time.

FÜSSEN

SCHOOL RULES

German schools only teach four or five classes per day. They usually dismiss at lunchtime. Students spend their afternoons doing homework and playing sports.

German children start school early. Most attend preschool starting at age 3. Primary school begins at age 6. Students choose a secondary school when they are 10. They can continue their general studies, prepare for work or university, or all three. All students must attend school until age 15 or 16.

Most German workers have **service jobs**. They work in areas like banking, government, or education. Others work in **manufacturing**. They make machinery, electronics, and cars. Volkswagen and Porsche are some of Germany's famous auto brands.

FIREFIGHTERS

Feuerwehr

CAR ENGINEERS

FUSSBALL

Tennis and *fussball*, or soccer, are popular sports in Germany. Fans love to cheer their favorite teams to victory. Germans enjoy being active, too. Hikers, cyclists, and mountain climbers explore the country's beautiful **terrain**. The cold seas attract surfers, and the snow-covered Alps are a wintry delight for bold skiers.

German **culture** is rich with the music of legendary **composers**, including Bach and Beethoven. Centuries of art fill the country's museums. Grimms' fairy tales, such as "Cinderella" and "Sleeping Beauty," come to life through events held throughout the Black Forest!

BEETHOVEN

SCHOKOLADE ESSEN

Schokolade Essen, or Chocolate Eating, is a favorite party game in Germany. Any number of people can play. A large chocolate bar is wrapped in thick layers of newspaper. It is placed on a cutting board with a butter knife and fork. A hat, scarf, and gloves are needed, along with a pair of dice.

How to Play:

1. Players sit in a circle and try to roll doubles on the dice. The first player to roll a double quickly puts on the hat, scarf, and gloves. They use the knife and fork to try to unwrap the candy bar and eat as much as possible. The other players continue to roll the dice.

2. As soon as someone else rolls a double, that player gets the hat, scarf, mittens, utensils, and chocolate bar. They try to eat the chocolate themselves.

3. The other players continue to roll and pass the bar until all the chocolate is gone. The winner is whoever eats the most chocolate!

tbratwurst
ger Art
rt sausage 3,50

#gerbratwurst
er Art
berlin sausage 4,50

kauer
d sausage 4,50

sekrainer
sausage 4,50

Kiesenboulette
Berliner Art
german meatball 4,-

Steak
würzig pikant
spicy steak

IT'S THE WURST

Germany is known for its hundreds of
different kinds of *wursts,* or sausages.
The most popular among Germans is
currywurst. This bratwurst is served with
curry-spiced ketchup.

German food is **hearty** and filling. Most Germans start
the day with fruit, **muesli**, and yogurt. A mid-morning
snack calls for a sandwich or cereal bar. The largest
meal is at midday. It usually features a main course of
meat such as sausage or *schnitzel*, which is breaded
pork or veal. This is served with noodles, potato salad, or
dumplings called *knödel*.

Late afternoon brings *Kaffee und Kuchen*, coffee served with pastries like apple strudel or layer cakes. A light evening meal often includes meats, cheeses, pickles, and bread.

SCHNITZEL

APPLE STRUDEL

BLITZ KUCHEN (LIGHTNING CAKE) RECIPE

This fast, easy recipe is perfect for Kaffee und Kuchen! Have an adult help you.

Ingredients:
1/2 cup butter or margarine
1 1/4 cups sugar
3 eggs
1/4 cup milk
1 1/2 cups flour
1 1/2 teaspoons baking powder
1/4 cup sugar mixed with 2 teaspoons cinnamon

Steps:
1. Let milk warm to room temperature. Preheat oven to 350 degrees Fahrenheit (177 degrees Celsius).

2. Place butter in small bowl and cover with wax paper. Warm in microwave for 40 seconds on "high" or until softened.

3. Measure sugar into large bowl. Pour in butter and blend together.

4. Use the wax paper to wipe melted butter from the microwave bowl onto the inside of a 9x13-inch baking pan. Sprinkle a handful of flour evenly along the bottom of the pan.

5. Add eggs, milk, flour, and baking powder to bowl. Mix well, smoothing out lumps.

6. Spread batter evenly into pan. Sprinkle cinnamon-sugar evenly on top.

7. Bake for 30 minutes. Let cool and cut into bars. Serve with jam or fresh fruit.

CELEBRATIONS

Celebrations fill the German year with color. In winter's final months, *Karneval* brightens spirits across the country. It brings joyful costume parties, parades, and bonfires. Germany's most famous festival is Oktoberfest. It is held in late September. People celebrate with food, drinks, and carnival rides.

Germany's national holiday is the Day of Unity on October 3. It celebrates the **reunification** of East and West Germany. On the night of December 6, St. Nikolaus fills good children's shoes with small gifts. This mix of modern **tradition** and ancient legend is part of what makes Germany so special!

OKTOBERFEST

SNOW MALLS

In town squares across Germany, *Christkindlmarkts* sell holiday food and gifts through December. Shoppers visit booths for hot drinks while musicians entertain under the cold, starry skies. The markets disappear by Christmas Eve.

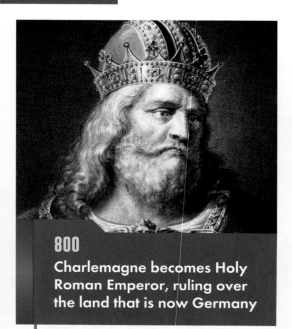

1914
World War I begins
when Kaiser Wilhelm II
declares war on Russia

800
Charlemagne becomes Holy
Roman Emperor, ruling over
the land that is now Germany

1517
Martin Luther leads the
Protestant Reformation,
a revolt against the
Catholic Church

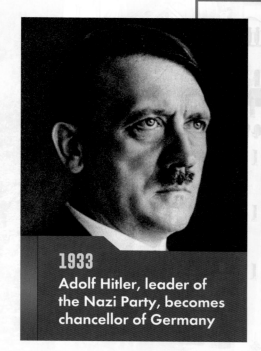

1933
Adolf Hitler, leader of
the Nazi Party, becomes
chancellor of Germany

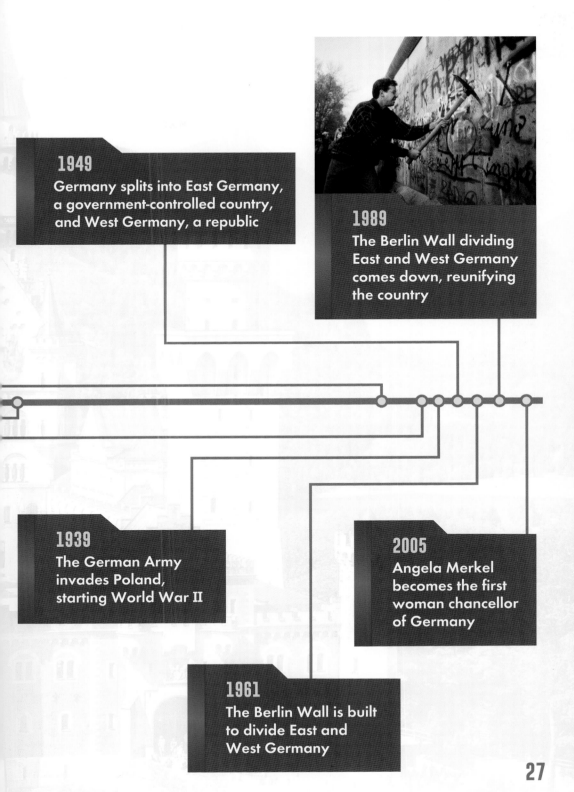

1949
Germany splits into East Germany, a government-controlled country, and West Germany, a republic

1989
The Berlin Wall dividing East and West Germany comes down, reunifying the country

1939
The German Army invades Poland, starting World War II

2005
Angela Merkel becomes the first woman chancellor of Germany

1961
The Berlin Wall is built to divide East and West Germany

GERMANY FACTS

Official Name: Federal Republic of Germany

Flag of Germany: Germany's flag features horizontal stripes of black, red, and gold. These colors were taken from the flag of the Holy Roman Empire, which featured a black eagle with red beak and claws on a gold background.

Area: 137,847 square miles
(357,022 square kilometers)

Capital City: Berlin

Important Cities: Munich, Hamburg, Cologne, Frankfurt

Population:
80,594,017 (July 2017)

WHERE PEOPLE LIVE

COUNTRYSIDE
24.7%

CITY
75.3%

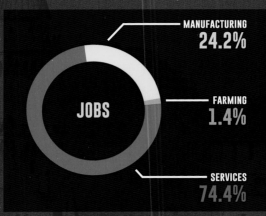

MANUFACTURING
24.2%

JOBS

FARMING
1.4%

SERVICES
74.4%

Main Exports:

 iron

 steel

 machinery

 vehicles

 electronics

National Holiday:
Unity Day (October 3)

Main Language:
German

Form of Government:
federal parliamentary republic

Title for Country Leader:
chancellor

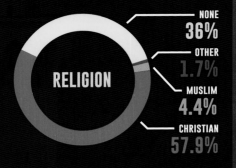

RELIGION

NONE
36%

OTHER
1.7%

MUSLIM
4.4%

CHRISTIAN
57.9%

Unit of Money:
Euro; 100 cents equal one Euro.

GLOSSARY

composers—people who write music

culture—the beliefs, arts, and ways of life in a place or society

dialects—local ways of speaking particular languages

elegant—of a high quality

hearty—plentiful and satisfying

hibernating—resting or sleeping through the winter

immigrants—people who move to a new country

manufacturing—a field of work in which people use machines to make products

marshes—wetlands that are filled with grasses

medieval—relating to the Middle Ages (500-1500 CE)

muesli—a granola-like cereal

native—originally from the area or related to a group of people that began in the area

plain—a large area of flat land

reunification—the act of bringing back together

service jobs—jobs that perform tasks for people or businesses

symbol—something that stands for something else

temperate—associated with a mild climate that does not have extreme heat or cold

terrain—the surface features of an area of land

tradition—a custom, idea, or belief handed down from one generation to the next

TO LEARN MORE

AT THE LIBRARY

Coddington, Andrew. *Germany.* New York, N.Y.: Cavendish Square, 2017.

Ganeri, Anita. *Germany.* Chicago, Ill.: Heinemann Raintree, 2015.

Grimm, Jacob and Wilhelm, and Margaret Hunt. *Gris Grimly's Tales from the Brothers Grimm.* New York, N.Y.: Balzer + Bray, 2016.

ON THE WEB

Learning more about Germany is as easy as 1, 2, 3.

1. Go to www.factsurfer.com.

2. Enter "Germany" into the search box.

3. Click the "Surf" button and you will see a list of related web sites.

With factsurfer.com, finding more information is just a click away.

INDEX

The images in this book are reproduced through the courtesy of: Canadastock, front cover, p. 9 (inset); Noppasin, pp. 4-5; RossHelen, p. 5 (top); Igor Plotnikov, p. 5 (middle top); LaMia Fotografia, p. 5 (middle bottom); ESB Professional, pp. 5 (bottom), 14; Brittany McIntosh, pp. 6-7, 8 (top); Juergen Wackenhut, p. 8; Outdoor Pixel, p. 9; Blickwinkel/ Alamy, pp. 10-11; All-stock-photos, p. 10 (top); Martin Pelanek, p. 10 (middle); Juan Martinez, pp. 10 (bottom left), 28 (flag); Nicram Sabod, p. 10 (bottom right); Markus Mainka, p. 12; 360b, p. 13 (top); TravelView, pp. 13 (bottom), 15; Westend61, p. 16; Sean Pavone/ Alamy, p. 17; Kzenon, pp. 18, 19 (top); Tim Graham/ Alamy, p. 19 (bottom); Chrisof Koepsel/ Stringer/ Getty Images, p. 20 (top); Look-foto/ Superstock, p. 20 (bottom); Georgios Kollidas, p. 21 (top); Gresei, p. 21 (bottom); Eden Breitz/ Alamy, p. 22; Tami Peterson, p. 23 (bottom); AS Food Studio, p. 23 (top); Elena Hramova, p. 23 (middle); Mirenska Olga, p. 24 (inset); S. Borisov, pp. 24-25; Everett Historical, p. 26 (top); Elzbieta Sekowska, p. 26 (bottom); Justin Leighton/ Alamy, p. 27; Alan Bauman, p. 29 (currency); Andrey Lobachev, p. 29 (coin).